TIME TRAVELING TO
1973
CELEBRATING A SPECIAL YEAR

TIME TRAVELING TO 1973

Author
Robert E. Miller

Design
Gonçalo Sousa

November 2022
ISBN: 9798365608351

Surprise!

Dear reader, thank you so much for purchasing my book!

To make this book more (much more!) affordable, the images are all black & white, but I've created a special gift for you!

You can now have access, for FREE, to the PDF version of this book with the original images!

Keep in mind that some are originally black & white, but a lot of them are colored.

Go to page 101 and follow the instructions to download it.

I hope you enjoy it!

Contents

We deliver fresh tomato flavor.
M'm! M'm! Good!

Chapter I: News & Current events 1973

Leading Events

The Watergate Scandal – January 1st to December 31st

Pres. Richard M. Nixon and Charles Wendell Colson

The Watergate Scandal began in June of 1972 when the Nixon government attempted to cover up its involvement in the break-in at the Democratic National Committee headquarters in Washington. After the five perpetrators were arrested, the US Justice department, and certain sections of the press, connected the money found on them to the Committee for the Re-Election of the President. The scandal became a huge story and by 1973 was dominating the news headlines.

By March, White House Counsel John Dean told Richard Nixon that there was 'a cancer' present in the presidency, and a month later he began to co-operate with the federal Watergate prosecutors.

In April the Senate Watergate Committee began its televised hearings where it was eventually established that the

Televised Watergate hearings

president had been aware of, and contributed to, the involvement of cover ups of the government's role in the break-in. The most telling evidence at that time was Dean's admission that he had discussed it with Nixon 'at least 35 times'. By this time, Dean had been fired from his position.

'The Saturday Night Massacre'

By July the pressure on the President was intense, as it had been revealed that all phone calls in the White House had been taped, but the president had refused to hand them over to the committee.

On October 20th, what became known as 'the Saturday Night Massacre' took place, when Nixon ordered cabinet members Elliot Richardson and William Ruckelshaus to fire special prosecutor Archibald Cox. They both refused and both resigned. In November, Nixon had addressed a huge American television audience and had stated that 'I am not a crook', but the scandal surrounding him continued. Although it was August 1974 before he finally made a resignation speech, the year of 1973 was a defining one in the history of American politics.

Richard Nixon sworn-in for second term as American President – January 20th

There can have been few other presidencies that were revolving around scandal as the one involving Richard Nixon, and as he was sworn-in on January 20th, 1973, for the second time, by Supreme Court Justice-in-Chief Warren Burger, his presidency was unravelling.

It seemed so far away from when the final vote count was made in 1972, as he took 61% of the popular vote, with his opponent George McGovern

President Richard Nixon is sworn in for a second term as First Lady Pat
Nixon holds the Bibles

on 38%. He won 521 college votes and carried 49 States, compared to
McGovern's 17 and two. It was clear that Nixon had gone into 1973 as a
very popular president, yet that was all to change.

US Involvement in The Vietnam War Ends – March 29th

The US-Vietnam War, which had raged for nearly 18 years, saw the
beginning of the end in 1973, as US involvement all but came to an end.
The process started on January 27th with the 'Paris Peace Accord'. The treaty
included the governments of the US, the Democratic Republic of Vietnam,
the Republic of Vietnam,
and the Republic of
South Vietnam.
The US ground forces,
who by now were
suffering low morale and
had effectively retreated,
were to be gradually
removed in the next
two-year period. The
time limit had been set

U.S. troops wading through a marsh in the Mekong delta,
South Vietnam

11

at sixty days for the US and its allies to withdraw, but this was optimistic. Unfortunately, the treaty was regularly broken by the north and south Vietnamese forces, but the desire of the American public to leave the war was so strong, that US forces played little part from that moment.

Sadly, the agreement continued to be ignored, but there was little response from the US government, enabling the communist control of Vietnam to escalate.

The aftermath saw a different view from historians. Many believed that the triangular agreement left South Vietnam totally isolated and alone, even though President Nixon had promised he would break the treaty should it be necessary. With his 'Watergate' scandal becoming increasingly more important during 1973, many believed that he had acted to court popularity.

Black September Group attack Athens Airport – August 5th

Athens Airport

The Black September Organisation was a group founded in 1970 by a Palestine militant faction. The name 'Black September' refers to the Jordanian Civil War in September 1970, which was regarded by Palestine as a black month.

The group had been responsible for terrorist attacks in the two years since they were formed, but the attack at Athens airport in August of 1973 was the most violent of its kind. Two Arabs, who had originally planned to hijack an aircraft, changed their minds when they saw the level of security, so instead decided to open fire on the passengers waiting at the departure lounge. In the mayhem that followed, they used machine guns and grenades, killing five and seriously injuring 55.

The attackers, Shafik el Arid and Tallal Khantouran, arrived in Athens with orders to attack any Israeli traveller. During this, they also held 35 hostages and kept the police at bay for two hours before being arrested. The Greek government had them tried and then sentenced to death in 1974, but that was then overruled and the two

'Black September', 1970

were deported to Libya, much to the anger of the Israeli government. The Black September group had already gained worldwide recognition after the Munich massacre at the 1972 Olympic Games, and they continued their terrorist activities right up until 1981, but by 1988 it was suggested that the organisation had been disbanded and were no longer active.

Other Major Events

The Supreme Court rules on Roe v Wade – January 22nd

An anti-abortion rally in New York City, 1973

This landmark case was decided on January 22nd, 1973, after nearly thirteen months of wrangling. The case was brought by Norma McCorvey – known as Jane Doe – against her Texas District Attorney, Henry Wade. McCorvey was pregnant with her third child in 1969 but wanted an abortion.

The problem was, she lived in Texas, where abortion was illegal. Her attorneys, Sarah Weddington, and Linda Coffee, filed a lawsuit on her behalf against Wade, saying that the abortion laws in Texas were unconstitutional. A special three-judge court heard her case and ruled in her favor.

Norma McCorvey, left, who was Jane Roe in the 1973 Roe v. Wade case, with her attorney, Gloria Allred

On January 22nd, the Supreme Court issued a decision that said that the 'Fourteenth Amendment to the United States Constitution' provides a 'right to privacy' and a right for a woman to choose an abortion.

The argument continued, not just in 1973, but for years afterwards. Despite a groundswell of legal opinion that the ruling should be overturned, in 1992 it was reaffirmed by the Supreme Court, but that ended in 2022 on June 24th, when the court ruled that the right to abortion was not 'deeply rooted in this Nation's history or tradition'. It was a shattering blow to pro-abortionists.

Boeing 707 crashes in Nigeria killing 176 – January 22nd

Crashed plane in Kano, Nigeria

A two-year-old Boeing 707 crashes whilst attempting to land at Kano airport in Nigeria. The plane, chartered by Nigerian Airlines, was flying back from Jeddah, and attempted to land in strong winds. It hit a depression in the runway and the nose wheel collapsed, forcing the aircraft to turn 180 degrees and quickly catch fire. 176 passengers were killed and there were 26 survivors.

Leonid Brezhnev becomes first Soviet leader to address the American public – June 24th

For a week in June, America hosted The Washington Summit, a meeting of the two world superpowers, the United States and the Soviet Union. The Cold War was at its height, and this was watched by the whole world. During the seven-day meeting, the 'Agreement on the Prevention of Nuclear War' was signed, signalling a new warmth between President Nixon and General Secretary Brezhnev. It was confirmed when Brezhnev was invited to make a live public address to the American people on both radio

Leonid Brezhnev

and television, the first such honour afforded a Soviet official. The address was watched and listened to by millions of people, not just in the US, but around the world. It was stilted and sometimes slow, as the translator at times struggled, but in essence Brezhnev had regarded the summit as a success, regretted that he hadn't had the opportunity of seeing more of America, and hoped that the peaceful negotiations would be a

The 1973 Agreement on the Prevention of Nuclear War

catalyst for the future. The speech lasted for 47 minutes and was a success. The next day, Brezhnev left the summit a day earlier than expected, and flew to Paris, where he met President Pompidou of France.

The Assassination of Spanish Prime Minister Blanco – December 20th

Luis Carrero Blanco

Luis Carrero Blanco was assassinated on December 20th, 1973, in what was regarded as the biggest attack against the Spanish Francoist state since the end of the Civil War in 1939.

The attack was committed by the Basque Separatist movement ETA and was planned with military precision. During 1973, the health of the Spanish dictator Francisco Franco had declined badly, and it was in this state that he was clinging on to the last vestiges of power. The left-wing and pro-Basque group looked upon the attack as a way of destabilising Spain and forcing the Basque residents to follow the 'lesser evil' of the terrorist group. It took place when members of the group rented a basement flat in Madrid and proceeded to dig a tunnel. This eventually ended under the exact sport where Blanco travelled on a daily basis to attend Mass at the San Francisco de Borja church. They packed the tunnel with 180Ib of explosives and detonated it at the time the convoy was travelling. The blast was so fierce that Blanco's car was sent over 60 feet into the air. The students, now dressed as electricians, shouted to passers-by that there had been a gas explosion, and in the mayhem that followed, they escaped.

Blanco wasn't killed immediately but was rushed to hospital where he succumbed to his injuries, some 39 minutes after the attack. His bodyguard and driver died shortly afterwards.

ETA Members

Rather strangely, the attack wasn't condemned quite as strongly as expected, as the exiled opposition party believed it was the only thing that ETA had done to move forward the process of Basque Independence, and the new Prime Minister, Torcuato Fernández-Miranda, refused to declare a State of Emergency.

ETA remained active until the second decade of this century, with over 800 killed in various attacks throughout the country, and finally ceased all actions in 2018.

Political Events

The UK, Ireland and Denmark enter the EC – January 1st

At the end of 1972, the European Community had just six members, Germany, France, Italy, Netherlands, Belgium, and Luxembourg, but by the start of 1973, that had been increased to nine as the United Kingdom, Ireland and Denmark all joined. The road to the EC for all three was a different one. The UK, still struggling with crippling debts following World War Two, looked to benefit from the economic freedom that could be

Otto Moller, left, Danish Ambassador in Brussels, hands his letter of credentials to André Dubois, Secretary-General of the Council of the European Communities

gained from European inclusion. Ireland, heavily dependent on the UK financially due to exports and imports, joined suit, whilst Denmark, who were a member of the Outer Seven (an economical group of countries not involved with the EC) wanted also to be involved.

Both Ireland and Denmark held referendums in 1972, where the result was an overwhelming approval to join, whereas the UK didn't actually go to the public until 1975.

Greenland withdrew in 1985, and the United Kingdom had a referendum and withdrew, from what is now called the European Union, on January 31st, 2020. The EU now has 27 member States, with Germany and France regarded as the strongest economically following the UK's departure.

The UK – Iceland 'Cod War' - September 1972 to November 1973

The UK frigate HMS Mermaid collides with the Icelandic Coast Guard Vessel Thor

The 'Cod Wars' between the two countries had actually been taking place for centuries, but in the 20th century hey became more pronounced. It was effectively the second 'Cod War' following a similar skirmish in 1958 that lasted for three years. On this occasion, Iceland increased their fishing rights to 50 miles off the coast, banning other nations – basically just the UK – from taking up valuable stocks. The UK contested this, citing an historical agreement from centuries before of their right to fish off the coast of Iceland.

In January, The Royal Navy was deployed to protect British fishing vessels, with the RAF flying above warning the boats as to where the Icelandic navy were. The Icelandic government was so incensed that prime minister Ólafur Jóhannesson asked the US to send aircraft to bomb the Royal Navy frigates. The US politely declined.

By this time, NATO was becoming increasingly nervous of a full-scale conflict between the two islands, and with the British having a far greater military presence, diplomatic meetings took place regularly in London and Reykjavik. During the course of the latest conflict, 32 Royal Navy frigates had

Prime Minister of Iceland, Ólafur Jóhannesson

entered the Icelandic waters to protect the trawlers and fishermen.

The second 'Cod War' was brought to an end once NATO had intervened and asked the British to withdraw their warships and frigates. An agreement to the amount of fish catch was made, with the British restricted to around 130,000 tonnes.

The end of the second dispute was seen by many as a victory for a small country over a powerful one, and there were celebrations in the Icelandic capital once it had been announced. The agreement came to an end in 1975, when, yes, the third 'Cod War' flared up!

The Yom Kippur War – 6th October to 25th October 1973

This was the fourth Arab Israeli war between Israel and a coalition of Arab States including Egypt and Syria. Most of the conflict took place on the Golan Heights, which in 1973 was occupied by Israel, and started on October 6th when the Arab coalition made a surprise attack on the day of Yom Kippur.

The war was part of the ongoing conflict that had started in 1948, following the founding of the state of Israel. During the 'Six Day War' in 1967, Israel had captured the Sinai Peninsula, and the territories of the West Bank. Despite a fragile peace, the skirmishes continued on a regular basis, with the two Superpower nations, the USA and the Soviet Union, backing their allies with weapons and financial aid.

In the week leading up to Yom Kippur, Egyptian forces were involved in a huge training exercise alongside the Suez Canal. This was monitored closely by Israeli intelligence, who at first dismissed them as mere exercises. Despite this, they deployed their own forces to the area.

One day before, Israeli General Ariel Sharon was shown ariel photographs of the forces at the border and was convinced that war was imminent. Syrian forces had joined with their Egypt allies and Soviet weaponry could be seen visibly. It was later that evening that all Israel reservists were called up, as

Clockwise from top-left: Israeli tanks crossing the Suez Canal; Israeli Nesher variant of the Mirage V fighter jet flying over the Golan Height; Israeli soldier praying in the Sinai Peninsula; Israeli troops evacuating wounded personnel; Egyptian troops raising the flag of Egypt at a former Israeli position in the Sinai Peninsula; Egyptian soldiers with a portrait of Anwar Sadat

intelligence suggested that an attack would take place at sunrise on October 6th.

The war started on the morning, when the Arab coalition launched their weapons against the Israeli-occupied Sinai on the left bank of the Suez Canal.

The superior US military equipment meant that soon Israel took command of the conflict and were able to cross the Suez Canal and surround the Egyptian Third

Israel Army General Ariel (center) and Defense Minister Moshe Day (right) during the Yom Kippur War.

Army and disable a large part of their Air Force too. The same story played out on the Golan Heights, despite heavy losses to the Israel army, and this led to the United Nations adopting Resolution 338, which demanded an immediate end to all hostilities. A formal ceasefire agreement was signed on November 11th.

The Mountjoy Prison Helicopter Escape – October 31st

The Mountjoy Prison helicopter escape, involving IRA members Seamus Twomey, Kevin Mallon, and Joe B O'Hagan, was an embarrassing moment for the Irish government. Fine Gael, the controlling party, had been attempting to curtail the activities of the IRA, as 'The Troubles' had become increasingly more violent. Most known members of Irish

An aerial of Mountjoy prison, 1973

Republican Army were arrested and sent to prison, but most also refused to accept the British orientated justice system.

On October 31st, helicopter pilot Thompson Boyes was introduced to man called 'Mr Lennard'. He said that he was a photographer and wanted to hire the helicopter to take ariel pictures of County Laois. He asked if they could firstly fly to Stradbally to pick up his equipment.

An Aérospatiale Alouette II, the type of helicopter used in the escape

Once they had landed, the pilot was greeted by two masked gunmen, and was told that he wouldn't be hurt if he followed instructions. From there, they flew to the prison, where Boyes was instructed to land in the exercise yard. Prisoners were enjoying their daily walk, and at first, the prison officers took little notice. They believed the helicopter was delivering Paddy Donegan, the Minister for Defence, who was due that day. It was only when the three IRA members, clambered into the helicopter, that the alarm was raised.

The three, with the gunman and the petrified pilot, then flew to a disused racecourse in Baldoyle, near Dublin. There they were put in waiting taxis and transferred to 'safe houses', whilst Boyes was released unharmed.

The government sent over twenty thousand officers into a huge manhunt across the country, and they were successful, as on December 10th, Kevin

Mallon was recaptured at a Gaelic Dance evening in Portlaoise. It took two years for O'Hagan to be recaptured, and Twomey managed to evade until 1977.

The aftermath of the escape in 1973, was that all IRA prisoners at Mountjoy Prison were moved to the maximum security of Portlaoise Prison with the Irish army guarding the inmates.

Other Notable Events

First Mobile Phone Call – April 3rd

Dr. Martin Cooper, the inventor of the cell phone, with DynaTAC prototype

With the mobile phone now part of everyone's lives, it's understandable to think that it is a recent technological advancement. It isn't. Can you believe that the first call on a mobile phone – or cell phone as it is referred to in the United States – took place on a New York Street in April 1973?

It was made by Motorola employee Martin Cooper on a prototype that would eventually become the DynaTAC 8000x and was made to his head office in New Jersey. That doesn't sound dramatic, but he was stood on Sixth Avenue in New York at the time.

Apparently, the conversation was rather bland and wasn't noted for posterity. It was later remembered as 'I'm ringing just to see if my call sounds good at your end', which with the greatest will in the world is hardly memorable. It doesn't compare with the first telegram – 'What God has wrought' – but it was certainly one of the most ground-breaking.

DynaTAC 8000x

Martin Cooper has almost been lost in history, but it was he who actually invented the mobile phone. He had joined Motorola in 1967 and was responsible for the invention of a cellular-like portable handheld radio system for the Chicago police department, and by 1970 was the head of the company's communication division.

The phone was as large as a brick and just as heavy, and in current terms it cost in the region of $1million, but it worked. Ahead of a press conference on April 3rd, he took a sceptical journalist outside onto the streets to show that it could work. It did, and the rest is history.

Vickers Vanguard aircraft crashed in Switzerland killing 108 – April 10th

In what had been a bad year for aircraft safety, this British Vickers Vanguard plane crashed into a forested hillside whilst approaching Basel airport in Switzerland. Of the 133 on board, 108 were killed, making it the worst accident on Swiss soil. It was said that the main pilot, Anthony Dorman, became disorientated, and his co-pilot, Ivor Terry, took over

Vickers Vanguard aircraft remains

the final approach but misidentified a landing beacon. The inquest suggested that the two pilots may have been confused by electricity lines that caused 'ghost' beacons to appear. Most of the passengers and crew were British, and the crash left 55 children motherless.

Concorde crosses the Atlantic in record-breaking time – September 26th

The British-French designed and built Concorde was the first supersonic passenger aircraft. It had the slogan 'Arrive before you leave', due to the fact it could travel at twice the speed of sound at around 1,400mph. Only 20

Concorde in flight, circa

were built, with the first being ready in 1969, but passengers were unsure as to how safe such a slim and unusual aircraft was travelling at such speeds. Both British Airways and Aerospatiale then went on a charm offensive and took the plane on numerous tours, including the United States.

By 1973, the companies were still looking for a passenger licence, so the French authorities decided to show how impressive the aircraft was by flying non-stop from Washington to Paris in record time. Pilots Jena Franchi and Gilbert Defer were given the task of making history. Along with a handful of passengers and crew, the plane arrived in Paris three hours and thirty-two minutes later, averaging 954 mph. It was impressive, but it still took another three years before the aircraft was allowed to fly commercially.

Soon Concorde was the only way any self-respecting millionaire would travel between the two continents. Actor Richard Harris once boasted of flying to New York for a lunch date with a female friend, before taking the return journey later that afternoon.

The aircraft had an exemplary safety record, but a crash on take-off in Paris in 2000, killed all 109 on board. Shortly afterwards, the planes were decommissioned and now sit in various museums in both the UK and France.

Netherlands introduces 'car-free' Sundays – November 5th

Cyclists, moped riders and a cargo bike on a car-free crossing, Amsterdam, 1973

As the oil and energy crisis hit the world in 1973, each country had their own way of dealing with it, and the Netherlands decided to introduce 'car-free' Sundays. It meant that city centres were quiet and full of bicycles, motorways were abandoned and there were lengthy queues for buses. It was broadly welcomed by the Dutch public, especially as emergency services and public transport were not part of the initiative.

There were extensive punishments for those who broke the ban, including a six-month prison sentence or a $20,000 fine (harsh in 1973), but few were caught. The ban lasted three months until the energy crisis began to recover.

Three-day working week introduced in the UK – December 17th

On December 17th, prime minister Edward Heath made the controversial decision to put the UK into a three-day working week. This was due to the cost of energy following a lengthy miners' strike earlier in the year. The measures were draconian as they included reduction of energy and electricity usage, blackouts in homes, schools and street lighting and television

stations being forced to end transmissions at 10.30pm each day. It was introduced on December 31st and lasted until February 8th, 1974. At that time a General Election was called, but it resulted in a hung parliament.

A telephonist works by torchlight at the start of the three-day week

Walkie-talkies most popular gift at Christmas – Christmas Day

Walkie-Talkie with Morse Code Transceiver

Amongst the Space hoppers, plastic model kits and vinyl records, the most popular Christmas Day gift in the USA and the UK in 1973 was a 'walkie-talkie'. These plastic communication devices, the forerunner of a mobile (cell) phone, were extremely popular due to the TV series 'Batman and Robin' in which they were used. They had been used extensively by the military in the Second World War and are still in operation today where the phone signal is limited. They had a limited range, and it wasn't clear if they served any really useful purpose except for children to use the 'over and out' farewell saying in dramatic style. There are no sales figures available, but manufacturer Motorola saw it as their best-selling item in the lead up to the festive season in 1973.

Chapter II: Crime & Punishment 1973

Major Crime Events

The 1973 Old Bailey bombing by the IRA – March 8th

1973 Old Bailey bombing

The Old Bailey bombing in London on March 8th, 1973, by the Irish Republican Army was dubbed 'Black Thursday' by the media newspapers. It was the first attack by the IRA on mainland England since 'The Troubles' had begun in the 1960s.

At the same time as the bomb went off outside the courthouse, another bomb was detonated in Whitehall nearby, with the result being that nearly 220 people were injured.

Up until this moment, England had been untouched by the terrorism that was spread over Northern Ireland by both the IRA and Loyalist groups but following an attack in Dublin by Loyalists in January 1973, where three civilians were killed, the IRA made the decision to target the mainland.

There were actually three targets, the Old Bailey, the Ministry of Agriculture in

Explosion of IRA car-bomb in progress

Whitehall and New Scotland Yard police station. The bomb at the latter was discovered by a police officer who noticed a car parked outside the building with an unusual license plate. As the British had been forewarned by the Royal Ulster Constabulary of a possible bombing campaign in England, a bomb squad was deployed. They found the explosive and managed to diffuse it before it could go off.

Unfortunately, the other two bombs did explode, causing serious damage. The ten men and women who were involved in the bombings were arrested at Heathrow Airport as their passports didn't match the names they had given, and the trial – switched from the damaged Old Bailey to Winchester – took nearly ten weeks. Eventually all were found guilty and sentenced to life imprisonment or twenty years, with the exception of Roisin McNeaney. She was acquitted after agreeing to turn informant on the IRA.

The bombing campaign of England continued in 1973, with the King's Cross and Euston train station bombings, injuring 13 people. That was followed by the Westminster bombing, where over 60 were injured and further attacks saw two people die.

Fred and Rose West continue their killing spree – April 20th to December 27th

Fred and Rose West are regarded as Britain's worst serial killers, kidnapping, raping, torturing and murdering a confirmed 12 victims over a 28-year

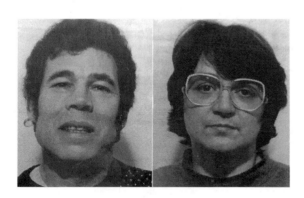

Fred and Rose West

period, although the real number is still unknown. On April 20th, they committed their first sexual murder, against lodger Lynn Gough aged 19. On November 10th, they murdered 15-year-old Carol Ann Cooper and on

December 27th, 21-year-old Lucy Partington. All the bodies were either buried under the house or in the back garden. The Wests started their murder spree in 1967 and continued until 1987, and it wasn't until 1994 that they were arrested and charged. Fred West then admitted that he was responsible for a further 18 murders, bringing the total to 30, but in 1995 he killed himself in prison. His wife Rose was sentenced to ten life term imprisonments.

The Kidnapping of John Paul Getty III – July 10th

John Paul Getty III was the grandson of oil tycoon John Paul Getty, once the richest man in the world, and his kidnapping by an Italian mafia organization in July, was headline news. Getty, who was 16, was staying in Rome with his girlfriend, and at

J. Paul Getty III

3am on July 10th, was kidnapped in the Piazza Farnese centre of the city. He was bound and gagged and taken in a car to the southern Italian town of Calabria. The kidnappers immediately released a statement saying they were holding Getty and demanded a ransom of $17 million. Getty senior refused to play along, mainly because the young Getty had frequently said to his girlfriend that he was going to arrange for his own kidnapping to make money. Both of them were struggling financially and his grandfather had refused to allow him any of his inheritance.

The kidnappers then sent a second demand, but in a ridiculous development, it didn't arrive in time as the Italian postal service was on strike! By this time, the treatment of Getty became worse. They killed a bird that he had befriended and played Russian Roulette with a gun, destroying the young boy's fragile mentality.

In November, a newspaper received an envelope that contained a letter and a human ear. The letter said, 'This is Paul's first ear. If within ten days the family still believes that this is a joke mounted by him, then the other ear will arrive. In other words, he will arrive in little bits.' There was also a further demand of $3.2 million.

By now, Paul's health had deteriorated so badly that he was given penicillin and brandy (he later attributed the amount of brandy to his alcohol addiction as he grew older), and the kidnappers now feared he may die. Eventually though, Getty paid £2.2 million, which was the most allowed that was tax deductible, and lent the remainder to his son, Paul's father. That had to be repaid at a four per cent interest rate too.

On December 15th, 1973, Paul was found alive at a gas station. His health was failing, but he was alive. His mother suggested that he should thank his grandfather for paying the ransom, but Paul refused to do so. Nine of the kidnappers were quickly arrested, but only two were charged, as the others were released due to a lack of evidence. The ransom money was never found.

J. Paul Getty III in his later years

Paul tried to rebuild his life, and after marrying, he had a child. Unfortunately, the kidnapping had affected him mentally and he became dependant on drugs and alcohol, and in 1981, after ingesting a combination of methadone, Valium, and alcohol, he became paralysed and unable to speak. He spent the rest of his life in a wheelchair. Paul died in 2011 at the age of 54.

Chapter III: Entertainment 1973

Silver Screen

George Lucas begins writing 'Star Wars' – January

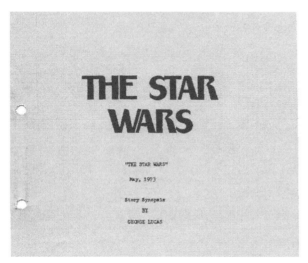

The Star Wars story treatment cover   George Lucas

The famous 'Star Wars' film franchise actually started to take shape in January 1973, when George Lucas began writing the script 'The Adventures of Luke Starkiller'. This was a 14-page draft, and it was completed by April, but it was thought to be too long for just one film, yet that didn't put Lucas off. He decided he wanted to make it into a trilogy, which eventually became a tri-trilogy, with nine films made into three different parts.

It wasn't initially successful as Lucas couldn't spell or introduce punctuation, so it was rejected by two major film companies. Only after his success at directing 'American Graffiti' did he manage to sell the idea to Twentieth Century Fox. The rest of course is history...

Top films of 1973

The Exorcist

In what was a bumper year for cinema in 1973, there is no doubt that there was one film that dominated, and that was the supernatural horror 'The Exorcist'. Directed by William Friedkin and starring Linda Blair and Max von Sydow amongst others, it was the talking point of the year, despite not being officially released until December in only 24 theaters in the United States.

Although it was immediately popular, many cinemagoers suffered trauma after watching it, others walking out due to the horrific nature of some of the scenes. It had quickly become extremely controversial.

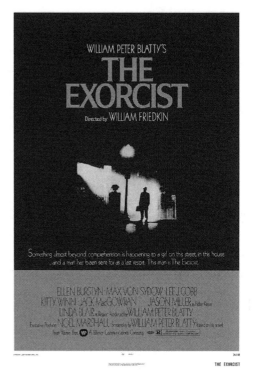

The Exorcist

Despite this, it was nominated for ten Academy Awards, winning two. The story was taken from the book of the same name from two years earlier and told of a young girl who is apparently possessed by a demon. Some of the scenes were so shocking that the Catholic Church expressed their concerns, yet within a week it had grossed over $2 million. Warner Bros then extended its release all over the country, and for the following year it became the highest earner around the world. It was also released in the UK and Europe in early 1974, where the reaction was as controversial.

Remaining Top Three Films

The Sting

Released on Christmas Day, 'The Sting' starring Paul Newman and Robert Redford instantly became one of the all-time classics. Set in 1936, it tells the story of two conmen, who invent an elaborate plot to con a mob boss, played by Robert Shaw. The film, directed by George Roy Hill, is based on a real-life story told in the 1940 book 'The Big Con. The Story of the Confidence Man'.

The Sting

The title of the film refers to the moment the conmen get the pay-off. The film plays out each level of the sting, with hundreds of people involved. The story saw a fake betting office created, gangster boss Doyle Lonnegan, betting on a horse, misunderstanding the vague instructions he had been given, and the eventual Sting.

The film had Newman and Redford reunited after they had appeared in 'Butch Cassidy and the Sundance Kid' a few years earlier, and their starring roles helped to sell the film. Despite it being released so late in the year, it took over $1.5 million in its first week, and eventually over $160 million. In 1974, it was awarded 'Best Film' at the Academy Award Oscar ceremony.

Papillon

Directed by Franklin J Schaffner, this Steve McQueen and Dustin Hoffman epic, grossed over $3 million in its first two weeks from its December release date. Due to it being filmed in numerous locations, it was one of the most expensive films at the time, but box office takings were double that.

The story is set in 1933 France, where McQueen's character – Henri Charrière – is wrongly convicted of murdering a pimp and is sent to a French Guiana penal colony for life imprisonment. There he meets Louis Dega, played by Hoffman, and an unlikely friendship is made, where the two attempt escape on numerous occasions.

Papillon

The film is based on the autobiographical book of the same name, written by Charrière in 1969, with the title 'Papillon' being the French word for butterfly. It was named such due to the butterfly tattoos Charrière had on his body.

Other Top Ten Films of 1973

Other films that just missed out on the top three in 1973, were 'Live and Let Die' starring Roger Moore as James Bond for the first time, and 'American Graffiti' starring Richard Dreyfuss and Ron Howard.

'Live and Let Die' was the eighth in the James Bond series, and the first to star Roger Moore, who had replaced Sean Connery. It was directed by Guy Hamilton and is regularly named as one of the most popular Bond

Live and Let Die

films of all time. This is due to the crocodile scene, where Bond has to jump across a pond, by using the heads of the crocodiles as if they were steppingstones. It was also one of the first James Bond films where black actors played a significant role, although the voodoo scenes were later criticised. The film was tremendously popular around the world and grossed in the region of $35 million. 'American Graffiti' was a coming-of-age comedy directed by George Lucas and made stars of the two unknown leads in Dreyfuss and

Howard. The film had immediate financial problems, and Universal Pictures were not happy with the finished product. They wanted to seriously edit the final version, but Lucas refused, and with the help of producer Francis Ford Coppola, attempted to buy back the rights for a representative fee. The film studio refused, but once Coppola's 'The Godfather' won awards at that year's Academy awards, they relented and only cut three small scenes.
'The Way We Were' was a romantic

American Graffiti

The Way We Were

comedy and was basically a platform for Barbra Streisand and Robert Redford (again). It was hugely successful, directed by Sydney Pollack and also provided the pop charts with a hit single, taken from the theme music to the opening credits. 'Magnum Force' was the second of Clint Eastwood's Harry Callahan movies, following on from 'Dirty Harry'. It introduced the famous line 'Go ahead punk, make my day' as Callahan aimed his pistol at a young criminal. It became one of the catchphrases of the year. 'Robin Hood', 'Paper Moon' and 'Serpico' made up the top ten. The first is now an almost forgotten American/British Walt Disney animated film, which turned the traditional characters into anthropomorphic animals, whilst 'Paper Moon' was a vehicle for the new and exciting talent of Tatum O'Neal (who won an Academy Award for best supporting actress) and her real-life father Ryan O'Neal. Set in 1936 and shot in black-and-white, it's a charming black comedy that has stood the test of time.

Charming couldn't be a word to describe the last film of the top ten. 'Serpico'. A perfect vehicle for the talents of Al Pacino, it tells the real-life story of American crime fighter Frank Serpico. It

Robin Hood

Paper Moon   Serpico

was a huge success and Pacino was nominated for Best Actor at the Oscars but missed out to Jack Lemmon.

🎬 Box Office Figures

The numbers.com Box Office figures of 1973* for Worldwide sales.
*Figures sometimes refer to assigned over the period of the film's release, as opposed to its release year.

Rank	Title	Date	Total Gross
1	The Exorcist	December 26th, 1973	$193,000,000
2	The Sting	December 25th, 1973	$159, 616 327
3	American Graffiti	August 11th, 1973	$115,000,000
4	Papillon	December 16th, 1973	$53,267,000

Rank	Title	Date	Total Gross
5	The Way We Were	October 19th, 1973	$49,919,870
6	Magnum Force	December 26th, 1973	$44,680,773
7	Live and Let Die	June 27th, 1973	$35,400,000
8	Robin Hood	November 8th, 1973	$32,056,467
9	Paper Moon	January 1st, 1973	$30,333,743
10	Serpico	December 5th, 1973	$27,274,150

Other Film Releases – Comedy/Fantasy/Drama

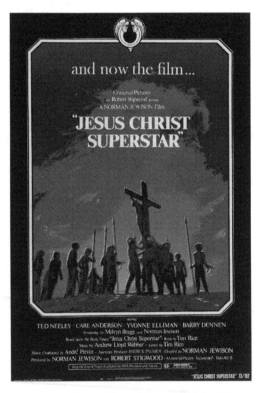

Jesus Christ Superstar

Not all films became huge Box Office hits at the time, but some stood the test and have become 'classics' since. One of those is 'Jesus Christ Superstar', which went on to gross over $24 million. An Andrew Lloyd Webber/Tim Rice-inspired rock opera, the film was directed by Norman Jewison. It was nominated for numerous Oscars but failed to win any. Telling the story of the 'Passion of Christ', it was a big budget epic that received mixed reviews. Many religious groups, including Catholics and Protestants were critical of the portrayal of Jesus Christ, whereas Pope Paul VI had a private viewing and loved every minute of it.

'Battle for the Planet of the Apes' was another film that struggled to receive instant recognition. It was probably due to the fact that as it was the fifth of the 'Planet of the Apes' franchise, cinema goers were becoming tired. Directed by J Lee Thompson and starring Roddy McDowell again, it received very negative reviews, with one going as far to say 'almost every line of the thin script attests the strain of having to find anything new for the apes to say or do.'

Battle for the Planet of the Apes

A Touch of Class

'A Touch of Class' was a British comedy starring Glenda Jackson and George Segal. It tells the story of a divorced British woman and a married American man, falling in love after an affair. The film was not expected to be particularly successful, but it was nominated for numerous Oscars, but won just one. That though, went to Jackson, who won Best Actress for her portrayal of Vickie Alessio. The film is now regarded as a classic in its genre. 'Sleeper' starring Woody Allen, was another film that seemed to get lost

Sleeper

amongst some of the great cinema of 1973. Set in a dystopian future of the United Staes, it tells the story of an owner of a health food store who is cryogenically frozen by accident in 1973, to be woken 200 years later in what had become a police-state.

The film received very positive reviews, with many comparing Allen's silent scenes as good as anything Buster Keaton had achieved in the age of the silent cinema.

Other Film Releases – 1973 – Sci-fi/Horror

There was very little in the way of Sci-fi in 1973, unless you include the already mentioned 'Planet of the Apes' franchise. Science fiction was not regarded highly at this time, and few would expect to make any money. 'Rollerball', 'Westworld' and 'Soylent Green' were the closest to Sci-fi in this year, but none of them really registered highly.

In the horror genre, as well as 'The Exorcist', the unique 'The Wicker Man' can be included. A relatively low budget British film, starring Edward Woodward and Christopher Lee, this

Rollerball

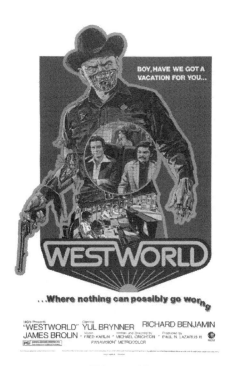

Westworld

Soylent Green

film arrived with a whimper in the UK cinemas, only for it to grow as the years passed and become one of the great classics of all time. Set on a Scottish Island, where pagan rituals dominate the lives of the citizens, it is played out to some wonderful Scottish folk music, with one of the most shocking endings to any film seen for some time. The cast of supporting characters included Britt Ekland and Ingrid Pitt, both to acclaim. Directed by Robin Hardy, it became even more famous many

The Wicker Man

years later, when deleted scenes were found near the building of a new motorway in England and were added.

Award Winners

The 30th Golden Globe Awards – Saturday, January 28th, 1973

🏆 **Winners**

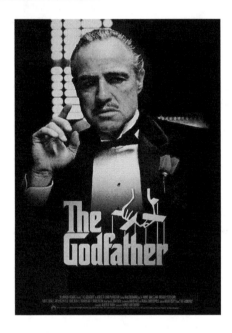

Best Motion Picture Drama
The Godfather

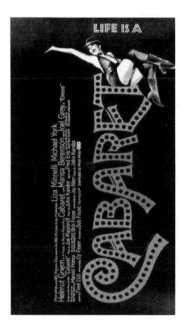

Best Picture Musical/Comedy
Cabaret

Best Actor Motion Picture Drama – Marlon Brando (The Godfather)

Best Actress Motion Picture Drama – Liv Ullman
(The Emigrants)

Best Actor Motion Picture Musical/
Comedy – Jack Lemmon (Avanti)

Best Actress Motion Picture Musical/Comedy
Liza Minelli (Cabaret)

Best Supporting Actor Motion
Picture Drama – Joel Gray (Cabaret)

Best Supporting Actress Motion
Picture Drama – Shelley Winters
(The Poseidon Adventure)

Best Director Motion Picture
Francis Ford Coppola
(The Godfather)

Best Screenplay – Francis Ford Coppola and
Mario Puzo (The Godfather)

The 26th British Academy Film and Television Awards – February 28th, 1973

🏆 **Winners**

Best Actor (Film) – Gene Hackman (The
French Connection/The Poseidon Adventure)

Best Actress (Film) – Liza Minelli
(Cabaret)

Best Supporting Actor – Ben Johnson
(The Last Picture Show)

Best Supporting Actress – Cloris
Leachman (The Last Picture Show)

Best Director – Bob Fosse (Cabaret) Best Original Music – Nino Rota
(The Godfather)

The 45th Academy Awards – Tuesday, March 27th, 1973 – Dorothy Chandler Pavilion, Los Angeles, California

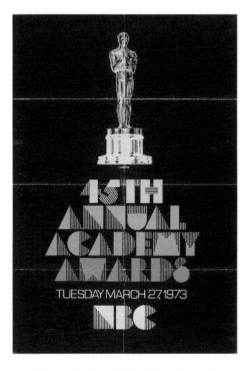

The 45th Annual Academy Awards

🏆 Winners

- 🏅 Best Actor in a Leading Role – Marlon Brando (The Godfather)

- 🏅 Best Actor in a Supporting Role – Joel Gray (Cabaret)

- 🏅 Best Actress in a Leading Role – Liza Minelli (Cabaret)

- 🏅 Best Actress in a Supporting Role – Eileen Heckart (Butterflies are Free)

- 🏅 Best Director – Bob Fosse (Cabaret)

- 🏅 Best Music (Original Score) – Charlie Chaplin/ Raymond Rasch/ Larry Russell (Limelight)

- 🏅 Best Music (Song) – Joel Hirschhorn/Al Kasha – The Morning After (The Poseidon Adventure)

- 🏅 Best Film – The Godfather

Top of the Charts

The Dark Side of the Moon – Pink Floyd

Pink Floyd

Released on March 1st, 1973, this was Pink Floyd's eight studio album, which quickly became their most successful. The idea behind the album was to try and explain the difficulties each member faced during their arduous lifestyle and dealing with mental health problems. The album is now one of the most critically acclaimed in the history of popular music, and regularly features in top ten listings. Estimated sales are in the region of 45 million, and it went platinum 14 times in the UK. In the US Billboard ratings, it charted for 962 consecutive weeks.

It took over nine months to record in London's Abbey Road Studios and also features one of the most original artworks on its cover, that of light retracting from a triangular prism. It was released in the UK two weeks after the US launch, and the group played it on their American tour, including a midnight performance at the Radio City Hall in New York in front of 6,000 fans.

Best Selling Albums of 1973

This is never regarded as an accurate list due to the complexity of counting the sales around the world, but bestsellingalbums.org believe they have managed to get as close as possible given the scarcity of reliable information.

Rank	Album Art	Album / Artist / Sales
1		Dark Side of the Moon – Pink Floyd (50,000,000 sales*)
2		Goodbye Yellow Brick Road – Elton John (31,000,000)
3		Tubular Bells – Mike Oldfield (18,000,000)

Rank	Album Art	Album / Artist / Sales
4		1967-1970 – The Beatles (14,400,000)
5		1962 – 1966 – The Beatles (13,300,000)
6		Houses of the Holy – Led Zeppelin (12,500,000)
7		John Livingstone Seagull Soundtrack – Neil Diamond (10,000,000)
8		John Denver's Greatest Hits – John Denver (9,800,000)

Rank	Album Art	Album / Artist / Sales
9		Greatest Hits – Janis Joplin (9,600,000)
10		Singles 1969-73 – The Carpenters (7,500,000)

*estimated

Best Selling Singles of 1973

This is open to argument, as singles in the USA far outstrip those elsewhere due to the sheer size of the population. For instance, 'Tie A Yellow Ribbon' is the best-selling single in the USA and the UK for 1973, yet 'The Show Must Go On' by Leo Sayer, a huge seller in the UK, is nowhere near the worldwide top ten. 'Crocodile Rock' by Elton John, 'You Are the Sunshine of My Life' by Stevie Wonder and 'Killing Me Softly' by Roberta Flack were

Tie A Yellow Ribbon

The Show Must Go On

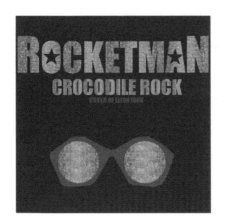

Crocodile Rock

You Are the Sunshine of My Life

Killing Me Softly

big-selling singles on both sides of the Atlantic. Figures are never accurate unfortunately, so I have returned to the same website to calculate the top ten.

🏆 Winners

1. Tie A Yellow Ribbon Round the Ole Oak Tree – Dawn featuring Tony Orlando
2. Bad, Bad Leroy Brown – Jim Croce
3. Killing Me Softly with His Song – Roberta Flack
4. Let's Get It On – Marvin Gaye
5. My Love – Paul McCartney and Wings

6. Why Me – Kris Kristofferson

7. Crocodile Rock – Elton John

8. Will It Go Round In Circles – Billy Preston

9. You're So Vain – Carly Simon

10. Touch Me In The Morning – Diana Ross

The 15th Annual Grammy Awards – March 3rd, 1973 – Tennessee Theatre – Tennessee

🏆 **Award Winners**

Record of the Year – The First Time Ever I Saw Your Face – Roberta Flack

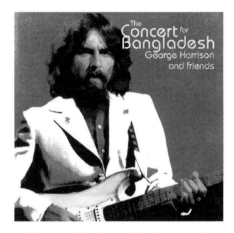

Album of the Year – The Concert for Bangladesh – Numerous Artists

Best New Artist – America

Television

Television in both the USA and the UK was widely different to today. In the UK there were only three channels, BBC1, BBC2 and ITV, and even they didn't broadcast all day. ITV came 'on-air' at 4pm and finished at midnight.

| BBC1 logo | BBC2 logo | ITV logo |

The BBC also ended their programmes at midnight and kept the tradition of playing 'God Save The Queen' at the close.

The United States was different, with many channels covering many areas, but ABC, CBS and NBC still dominated. 1973 saw many new programmes premiere, and some have lasted until almost today.

| ABC logo | CBS logo | NBC logo |

The Last of the Summer Wine – January 4th

'The Last of the Summer Wine' was broadcast for the first time in 1973 in the UK and became the longest running comedy series in history, finally ending in 2021. It was a weekly 30-minute gentle comedy set in the Yorkshire countryside and told the story of three retired older men who would just walk through around get into all kinds of 'adventures. The three characters changed as the years passed, but the story remained the same. It was hugely popular, with 'Nora Batty's stockings' a running gag throughout its run.

The Last of the Summer Wine

Elvis Presley – Aloha from Hawaii – January 14th

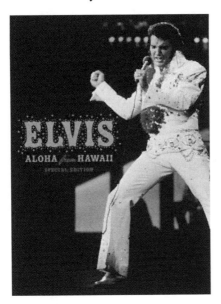

Elvis: Aloha from Hawaii

'Aloha from Hawaii' was an Elvis Presley concert that was broadcast live via satellite to Asia, but later delayed to both the US and Europe. When it was shown by NBC in the US on April 4th, it was their highest ratings program of the year. The delay was caused by the Super Bowl and the 'Elvis on Tour' film that had been released in cinemas. It is believed that around 1.3 billion people around the world eventually watched the concert either live or in the cinemas.

The Johnny Carson Show – Uri Geller embarrassment – November 8th

In the USA, 'The Johnny Carson Show' was one of the most watched in the country, a program that first aired in 1962 and carried on for thirty years. It was on this show that an embarrassing moment took place. On November

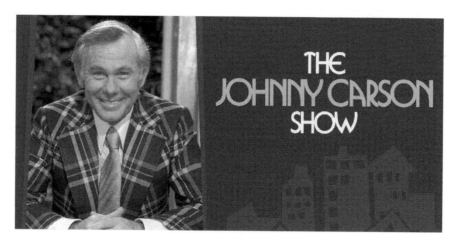

The Johnny Carson Show

8th, Carson invited magician and 'mind reader' Uri Geller to perform some of his favorite tricks to impress the audience. Carson was a former magician himself, so he was intrigued as to how effective Geller was. For that reason, he brought his own 'props' instead of letting Geller use his. What followed was thirty minutes of the most cringeworthy television ever seen.

Uri Geller bending a spoon

Geller spent some time with his hand hovering over metal thimbles in an attempt to see which held water. Each time, with the quiet encouragement of Carson, he failed and blamed it on his mind not being quite aligned to the task. Then, after many awkward silences and a few giggles from the live audience, he was asked to bend a spoon using his mind – the one trick that he had become famous for. He was unable to do that sufficiently, and at the end of the show, a clearly irritated Carson ended the segment. Geller then spent some time afterwards trying to sue the producers and consultant James Randi, but with no success.

The 30th Golden Globe Awards – Saturday, January 28th, 1973

Best Drama Series – Columbo

Best Musical/Comedy Series – M*A*S*H

Best Television Motion Picture –
That Certain Summer

Best Actor Drama Series – Peter Falk
(Columbo)

Best Actor Musical/Comedy Series
– Redd Foxx (Sanford and Son)

Best Actress Musical/Comedy Series
– Jean Stapleton (All in the Family)

The 26th British Academy of Film and Television Awards – March 27th, 1973

🏆 Winners

Best Actor – Anthony Hopkins (War and Peace)

Best Actress – Billie Whitelaw
(The Sextet)

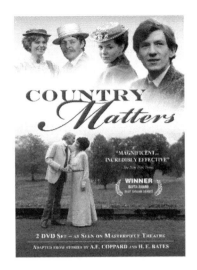

Best Television Series Drama or Serial
– Country Matters

Best Television Light Entertainment
Performance – Morecambe and Wise

Best Light Entertainment Programme – Monty Python's Flying Circus

Chapter IV: Sports Review 1973

American Sports

Super Bowl VII – Los Angeles Memorial Coliseum – January 14th

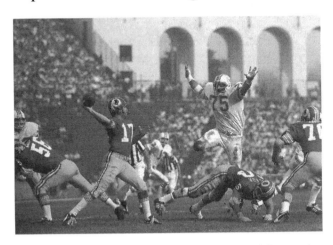
Super Bowl VII in 1973 at the Los Angeles Memorial Coliseum

Super Bowl VII, played at the Los Angeles Memorial Coliseum for the second time, saw the Miami Dolphins beat the Washington Redskins by 14 points to 7, and so become the first team in American Football to complete a full season undefeated.

The temperature on the day was in the high 80s Fahrenheit, making it the warmest Super Bowl to date, which probably accounts for the low-scoring nature of the game. It was also the first Super Bowl to be televised live in the city in which it was taking part. This had been blocked traditionally so as not to affect tickets sales, but the Los Angeles Coliseum sold out within days.

Jake Scott was the MVP of the game, and the whole contest saw just three touchdowns – Howard Twilley and Jim Kick for Miami, and Mike Bass for Washington. The traditional White House visit for the winning team didn't take place that year either, due to the Watergate Scandal which was becoming headlines news in the USA and around the world.

70th Edition of Baseball's World Series – October 13th to 21st

The Oakland A's world champion

The Oakland Athletics beat the New York Mets by 4 to 3 in the best-of-seven series, to win their second of three consecutive World Series titles. They were down by one going into the final two games, but their brash play (which matched their colorful uniforms and their colorful behaviour off the pitch) ensured another title.

Each game was played in the evening and each in front of a crowd of around 50,000. Game two was notable for the fact that the great Willie Mays recorded the final hit of his career.

Secretariat completes the Triple Crown – June 9th

Record-shattering Secretariat

It wasn't just that this wonder horse won the Belmont Stakes, as it was the firm favorite, but the manner in which it won. With only five horses in the field, jockey Ron Turcotte, knew that his horse was easily the favorite to win, but he could never have imagined that it would stroll home 31 lengths clear of the next! This was the largest margin of victory in Belmont history, and the time of two minutes and 24 seconds still stands as an American record for one and a half miles on dirt.

Secretariat was regarded as one of the greatest horses in the history of the sport, and by winning the Kentucky Derby and the Preakness Stakes, he became the first horse in 25 years to win the Triple Crown. In 1974 he was inducted into the Thoroughbred Horse Racing Hall of Fame. The horse lived until he was 19 and died in 1989, and still is regarded as the greatest by horse racing experts.

British Sports

92nd FA Cup Final – Wembley Stadium, London – May 5th

Sunderland's captain Bobby Kerr held aloft by his teammates Billy Hughes and goalkeeper Jim Montgomery

The FA Cup Final of 1973 has been recorded as one of the greatest upsets seen at the famous old stadium. Second Division Sunderland faced the might of one of the strongest teams in the land, Leeds United, and beat them 1-0. The image of Sunderland manager Bob Stokoe running across the pitch at full time to embrace Jim Montgomery has now become famous in the English game.

The reason why Montgomery was singled out for such praise and elation, was because as the goalkeeper, he had made some world class saves to keep Leeds at bay, following Ian Porterfield's goal in the first half. Sunderland held on and became the first Second Division team to lift the Cup since

West Bromwich Albion in 1931. One final note. The 1973 Final was the last time an orange ball was used, and now all finals use a traditional white ball.

England fail to qualify for the World Cup – October 17th

Peter Shilton could not bear to watch Allan Clarke's penalty

The night of October 17th has gone down in England footballing history as one of the most disastrous. It was simple. England, who had struggled in their qualifying group, had to beat Poland at Wembley to make the finals held in West Germany the following year. Bearing in mind they had won the tournament in 1966 and were one of the best teams in the world in 1970, failure to qualify was inconceivable. It happened though.

The story of the night was the Polish goalkeeper, Jan Tomaszewski. Branded by Brian Clough (one of the most famous English managers in the game) as a 'clown with gloves on', the 6' 4" keeper brilliantly save to deny what should have been a comfortable England victory. The home side had 36 shots on goal to Poland's two, hit the woodwork four times, cleared off the line twice and had a goal disallowed, but only a penalty gave England a 1-1 draw. It was Poland who qualified and not the 1966 World Champions. Even more remarkable was that Tomaszewski had played the game with five broken bones in his hand after an accidental kick from Allan Clarke.

Afterwards, the England manager Sir Alf Ramsey was sacked, and England then failed to qualify for the 1978 World Cup too. Meanwhile, Poland finished third in 1974.

International Sports

Five Nations Rugby Championship – January 13th to April 14th

The Five Nations championship

For the only time in the history of the Championship (including the later Six-Nation's version) the title was shared by all five nations, England, Scotland, Wales, France and Ireland. All teams won their two home matches, so of course lost their two away. Due to the troubles in Northern Ireland, neither Wales nor Scotland would play in Ireland, but England did. Despite an overwhelming victory for Ireland in the game (18-9), the English were applauded off. Afterwards the England captain, John Pullin, remarked that they may not have been very good, but at least they'd turned up!

George Foreman v Joe Frazier – Jamaica – January 22nd

Joe Frazier (left) and George Foreman during their weigh-in

The 'Sunshine Showdown' as it was billed was a heavyweight title bout between the two best boxers in the world in 1973. It took place in Kingston, Jamaica on January 22nd, 1973, and saw two fighters who had won 66 bouts between them, and no losses, play to a worldwide audience. Sadly, the spectacle was not quite what was hoped for as the fight only lasted one and a half rounds as Foreman won a technical knockout to become the new Heavyweight Champion of the World.

In the four and a half minutes of the showdown, Foreman knocked Frazier down SIX times before it was stopped. He went on to successfully defend his title twice, before losing to Muhammed Ali in the famous 'Rumble in the Jungle' in 1974.

The 87th Wimbledon Championships – June 25th to July 8th – All-England Club

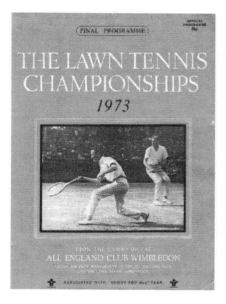

1973 Wimbledon Championships
Final Programme

The 1973 Wimbledon Championships was notable due to the act that 81 of the top men players in the world, including reigning champion Stan Smith, boycotted the event. It was following a suspension handed out to Yugoslavia's Nikola Pilic by the ILTF after it was reported he had refused to play in the Davis Cup. This was reduced to one month on appeal, but it meant he would have to miss Wimbledon. That then brought about the boycott.

It gave a lot of the unseeded players a chance of glory, and it was the Czech player Jan Kodes who took the men's title, beating Alex Metreveli in straight sets. One of the favorites, Ilie Nastase, who had defied the boycott, lost in the fourth round to a lesser player, and it was suggested that he deliberately 'threw' the match in support of the absent players. He has never commented on the accusation. In the women's singles, which was at full strength, Billie Jean King defeated Chris Evert in straight sets.

Roger Williamson is killed at the Dutch Grand Prix – July 29th

The fatal accident

The accident that took place on the eighth lap of the 1973 Dutch Grand Prix is one of the most horrific in the history of motor-racing, even by the standards of the 1970s. Williamson was competing in only his second F1 Grand Prix, and at a track that had gone through enormous safety updates, yet when his tyre burst at a fast corner, his car flipped upside down and there was no escape.

It has been established since that Williamson was alive when trapped in the car, which very quickly became a fireball as the leaking petrol ignited. The marshals were both poorly equipped and trained and had no idea how to deal with the inferno, and it was left to fellow British driver David Purley to try and rescue Williamson. He had stopped immediately on seeing the accident, but every other driver had continued racing, as was expected in those days. The images are shocking, especially the helpless Purley pleading with others to help him.

Purely was awarded the George Medal for bravery, and the Dutch circuit of Zandvoort went through yet more safety upgrades. At the end of the season, Jackie Stewart, who had just won his third World Championship, retired before the final race after seeing his teammate Francois Cevert killed in a practice accident.

Chapter V: General 1973

Pop Culture

**Novella 'Seagull' hits top of the book sales charts, stays for 40 weeks –
January 1973 onwards**

Jonathan Livingston Seagull

It was only in 1973 that this famous novella became such an international hit. Fully titled 'Jonathan Livingston Seagull', it tells the story of a seagull who is trying to learn about flight and life, and many see it as one of the first ever self-help books.

Written by Richard Bach and published in 1970, the book had little immediate impact, only selling in the region of 3,000 copies. Within a couple of years, word-of-mouth, had increased the print run to over 400,000 and in 1973 it stood atop the New York Times Bestseller list, where it stayed for an incredible 40 weeks. Booksellers didn't know how to classify it, so it was never seen in the same department at different shops, but it was the one novel that virtually everyone wanted. It became the best-selling book worldwide in 1973, and in the same year, a film version was made. The story was inspired by a real-life Jonathan Livingston. He was a test pilot who died from a heart attack after test flying a home-built Pitts Special.

Record attendance at Summer Jam Rock Festival – New York – July 28th

Summer Jam Rock Festival, 1973

The Watkins Glen raceway – home of the United States Grand Prix - was the venue for the Summer Jam Rock Festival, which recorded the highest ever attendance for such an event, at 600,000 visitors. 150,000 advance tickets had been sold, but far more arrived than expected, causing 8-mile traffic jams leading to the raceway. The two-day concert was thankfully without any major disturbances, but a skydiver crashed into the woods after the flares attached to his suit burst into flames.

The concert was regarded as a huge success, with the Grateful Dead playing the headline act, but due to the sheer numbers of people who attended, causing widespread disruption, it wasn't organised again at Watkins Glen until 2011.

Technological Advancements

The 'Big Ear' begins its search for extra-terrestrial life – January 1973 onwards

The Big Ear

The Ohio State University Radio Observatory – or the 'Big Ear' as it was commonly known - had opened in 1961 after five years of construction. Its main reflector measured

103 meters by 33 meters and was finely tuned to detect sounds from outer space. It was the first sky survey that searched for sounds of an extra-terrestrial nature. Although it didn't make any major discoveries in 1973, two years later it heard the Wow! Signal, which suggested it had come from the constellation of Sagittarius.

Sadly, the whole area was decommissioned in 1998 and abandoned, to be bought by a property developer who expanded a gold course on the site.

Xerox Alto computer introduced – March 1st

Xerox Alto I (1973) CPU with monitor, mouse, keyboard, and 5-key chording keyset

Ten years before mass marketing of computers became widespread, the Xerox Alto was introduced and became a hit with Silicon Valley. It was designed to support an operating system based on a graphical user interface. It was first seen in March of 1973, and initially only a handful were available. It was also the computer that Steve Jobs used to introduce Apple executives to its format, in return for Xerox to purchase stock options in the Apple company. The computer was ground-breaking and seen as the future of the technology business. It was a small device, and because only one person at a time could use it, the term 'personal computer' was also used for the first time.

Skylab launched into space – May 14th

The first United States space-station, Skylab, was launched on May 14th, 1973, with the help of a Saturn V moon rocket, that was equipped with habitat and workshop decks. The launch took place from NASA's Kennedy Space Center, with the goal to understand the effect of living in space on the human body. The launch wasn't without its hitches, as severe damage took place, including the loss of important solar panels. This meant that the

Skylab

lab lost a significant portion of its power throughout its life in space. There were three crews assigned to visit the space station on separate occasions throughout 1973 and into 1974, the first blasting off just eleven days later atop a Saturn 1B. Their mission was to complete extensive repairs to the station, which involved introducing a parasol-like sunshade, that would bring the temperatures down to an acceptable condition for habitat. This first manned crew of astronauts Pete Conrad, Joseph P. Kerwin and Paul J. Weitz stayed for a total of 28 days, and also became the first space-station occupants to return to earth safely.

A second crew were launched on July 28th and stayed for 59 days, where they performed scientific and medical experiments, whilst the third blasted off on November 16th, 1973, and surpassed all other by staying in space for 84 days. During the expeditions, Skylab orbited the earth 2,476 times. Eventually the funding for the space station stopped, as NASA was now concentrating almost entirely on the new Space Shuttle, so in 1979 it was abandoned and left to decay in space.

Wabot 1 – World's first humanoid robot invented – September 5th

Wabot – 1 was the first fun-scale anthropomorphic robot developed in the world at Tokyo's Waseda University. It consisted of a limb control, vision, and conversation system. It was able to communicate in Japanese and able to measure distances and directions. It walked with its lower limbs and was able to grip objects with its hands. It was estimated it had the mental faculty of a one and half year child

WABOT-1, 1973

Westworld becomes the first film to use DIP – November 21st

The futuristic film 'Westworld' starring Yul Brynner, was not only a hugely successful SciFi film set in a wild-west theme park, where the cowboys, played by robots, become out of control and start shooting the participants, but it was also the first film in history to use the new Digital Imaging Processing.

Director Michael Crichton originally went to the Jet Propulsion Lab in Pasadena, but after learning that two minutes of animation would cost $200,000, he contacted John Whitney Jr. He in turn went to Information International Inc., where they could complete the animation both faster and cheaply. Whitney Jr. digitally processed motion picture photography to appear pixelated in order to portray

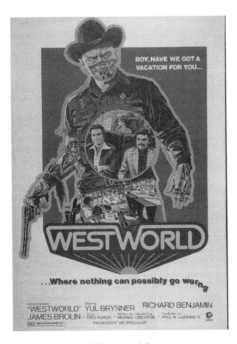

Westworld

the Gunslinger android's view. The 2 minutes and 31 seconds' worth of film was accomplished by colour-separating each frame of 70mm images, scanning each of these elements to convert into rectangular blocks, then adding colour. The resulting coarse pixel matrix was put back into the film. This is now a regular procedure, although the technology has far surpassed anything from 1973. 'Westworld' was a huge hit.

Fashion

Fashion photo session, 1973

There were some contrasts in fashion in 1973, but by far, the most popular was the hippie look, with colorful patterned clothing, hip huggers, bell bottoms, clogs, gypsy dresses, and tie-dye t-shirts. Crocheted clothing items were popular, along with denim, and hair was typically styled as long, or afro styled.

On the other side of fashion styles were the knitted sweaters, which led to sweater dresses, coats, and suits. Collars of coats were often fur-trimmed, the most popular being fox fur. Cardigans were popular, especially those with a belt, and they were typically chunky in neutral colors such as white and brown.

Men's Cacharel sweater, 1973

Simplicity 1973 Vintage
Sewing Pattern

At this time, fabrics and raw materials were suffering a shortage, so synthetic materials like nylon and vinyl became more prevalent in clothing. As for popular patterns and fabrics, checks, stripes, tweeds, plaids, and flannels were everywhere. The favorite color story of the time included pistachio, tangerine, peach, forest green, rust, and copper.

Although accessories were still being used, they were a little more subdued than in previous decades. However, rhinestone jewelry was making a comeback, and women (and men) still favored golden chains and earrings. The most significant change in women's fashion had more to do with hairstyles. The page boy cut was popular, and shorter hair with bangs was more the trend. For hippie styling, women's hair was typically long, straight, and parted in the middle. Men's facial hair included beards and mustaches and mutton chop sideburns.

1973 Sarah Coventry Jewelry
Collection April cover

For those who wanted a more polished look, dresses and skirts were resembling the fashions of the 1940s and 1950s. Skirts were often A-line or pleated and paired with buttoned tops. The necklines of dresses were pretty modest, with mandarin collars, pussy bow neckties, or large collars.

Chanel Dress Designed by Gaston
Berthelet for Chanel, Fall-Winter

Other popular clothing items were peasant blouses with wide sleeves, miniskirts, midi skirts, and dresses. Some skirts and dresses were ankle length and were often complemented with a macrame belt or a belt that matched the fabric.

Hush Puppies Shoes Advertisement

For shoes, popular choices were Hush Puppies, clogs, boots, sandals, Earth shoes, Wallabies, or waffle stompers. Earth shoes were soft-soled shoes and were named as such because they were supposed to connect the wearer with the Earth's electromagnetic field. Waffle stompers were a type of ankle-high hiking boots with big heavy soles, and they got their name from the noise they made when walking.

Glam Rock Style

In Britain, fashion had become androgynous, and the glam rock style was mainstream for both men and women. Popular were Western shirts with embroidery, tartan, velvet sports coats, frilly shirts, satin fabrics, leather jackets, ascots, and silk scarves. Drainpipe trousers were trendy, and platform shoes were a must. Most of the fashion trends came from music stars such as David Bowie, Kiss, and the Bay City Rollers.

Cars

1973 was a year of gas-guzzling oil-sapping cars, mostly in the United States. Whereas the rest of the world, especially in the UK and Europe, were looking at the oil crisis and building smaller cars, vehicles in America just got bigger.

The Cadillac Eldorado first sold in 1952, was still one of the most popular luxurious cars on the market. You could buy it as either a 2-door coupe or convertible, and to prove its desirability to the general public, it was chosen as the official pace car for the Indianapolis 500 race in 1973.

1973 Cadillac Eldorado Coupe

It had a top speed of 117 mph, 0-60 in a steady 9.7 seconds, and guzzled fuel at 9.4 mpg. It was a huge success though, and one-sixth of all Cadillac sales were the Eldorado.

1973 Buick Riviera

The General Motors Buick Riviera was their attempt to capture the luxury market. This car came as a two-door hardtop, yet sales were disappointing. By 1971 only around 31,000 cars had been sold, so a major relaunch was needed, with new bumpers and headlights to make the car look altogether more streamed. There was also the problem of the new safety measure – the 5-mph impact legislation – which made sure that a minimal impact would have no bearing on the structure of the front of the car. Like the Eldorado, the Riviera went through many generations of changes as the years passed.

The Pontiac Grandville was a full-size car that enjoyed enormous success and popularity prior to 1973, but once the fuel shortages and the oil crisis took effect, sales plummeted. The 455 cubic inch V8 engine was extremely thirsty, and these cars were seen more as status symbols as opposed to anything practical.

1973 Pontiac Grand Ville]

1973 Ford Cortina Mk III

In the UK and Europe, the Ford Cortina was the family car that everyone had to have, and for that reason was the best-selling car of the decade. The Mark III version, which could either be a saloon, estate, or two-door coupe, was built in England and also in South Africa, and dominated the roads. A 1300cc or 1600cc version was available, and with the heritage of Cortina success on the racetrack, it served as an all-purpose car for family's and youngsters alike.

Following on behind the Cortina was the Ford Escort and the ever popular Mini. The Escort was a smaller car that came with numerous engine sizes and different designs but remained popular right through until the end of the century. The fact that a version won the 1970 London to Mexico Rally, gave it the reputation of a wolf-in-sheep's-clothing image. Of course, the same could be said for the Mini…

1973 Ford Escort 1600 Mexico

On British roads for over a decade, the trendy Mini was everywhere, but as 1973 arrived, it started to look dated and slow compared to the newer models from Ford. Still with a 4-speed manual gearbox, engine sizes of 800cc, 1000cc and top of the range 1200cc, the car with four wheels at its four corners, was a joy to drive and as popular as ever, but production difficulties meant that its sales were gradually declining. It carried on in a new guise at the turn of the 21st century and is still a popular car in the UK today.

Popular Recreation

Anti-Monopoly board game

A popular board game in 1973 was 'Anti-Monopoly,' a game that was the complete opposite of the original Monopoly. It was created by a San Francisco State University professor who believed the original game encouraged monopolization. The Anti-Monopoly game starts as though a game of Monopoly has been completed, and instead of having public utilities and real estate for sale, the properties are individual businesses. Each player takes a role of a federal case worker and brings indictments against the businesses that have been monopolized to try and return the board to a system of free marketing. Sounds confusing, right? But it was the most popular board game of the year!

Another popular item of 1973 was the Raleigh Chopper bicycle. In the 1970s alone, it sold 1.5 million bicycles. Dungeons and Dragons were popular, along with Shrinky Dinks, first sold in 1973. Each Shrinky Dink set was comprised of thick sheets of polystyrene plastic that could be decorated and then baked in the oven, where they would shrink. They could then be used as charms or toys to play with.

Raleigh Chopper Mark2

Atari released Space Race in the summer of 1973 and has the honor of being the first racing game ever made. Although it wasn't the most complex of games created, there weren't that many around to compare it to in 1973. The

Space Race Atari

aim of the game is to get from the bottom of the screen to the top without striking dashes that represent asteroids.

The Six Million Dollar Man

If you were a kid or even an adult in 1973, you knew about The Six Million Dollar Man. A hit television series, it was a combination of science fiction and action. Lee Majors played the role of Steve Austin, a former astronaut who was rebuilt after an accident with bionic parts, super strength, and enhanced vision and speed. In 1975, an action man was created as merchandise which stood 13 inches tall and represented Steve Austin dressed in the red tracksuit he was often seen in on the program.

Another popular toy released in 1973 was the Baby Alive doll. It was the first of its kind that could eat, drink, and wet its pants. You could buy special packets of food that you mixed with water and feed the doll, which it would then chew and pass out the other end. It was a significant hit, particularly with little girls who felt they had their own babies to look after.

Arcade and video games were increasingly popular, with the likes of Pong, Super Soccer, Asteroid, Pro Tennis, and Gotcha among the most favored. In the Gotcha game, two players move through a continually changing maze,

1973 Baby Alive doll

Gotcha video game

with one player the pursued and the other the pursuer. The point is for the pursuer to catch the pursued, and as one gets nearer the other, an electronic beeping sound is emitted. It may not sound too exciting now, but in 1973, it was a new technology that had never been seen before, so it was exciting, and everyone wanted to play.

One of the most popular activities for adults in the 70s was the disco. Infamous Studio 54 was the hip place to be in New York, and it was normal to run into celebrities hanging out there most nights. Disco wasn't just a nightclub thing, though; there were many roller disco locations around, too. That way, you could combine the fun and music of disco with roller skating.

Crowds line up for entry into Manhattan's renowned disco and nightclub Studio 54, located at 254 West 54th Street

Drive-in Movie

Other popular pastimes of adults included going to a drive-in movie, especially for couples or those on their first date. Bowling was another popular activity, and

Bowling

Fondue party

for some, it became a real passion, and workplaces and social groups often had bowling leagues so they could meet regularly and compete against each other.

Finally, perhaps the most common social activities were the cocktail or fondue parties. Women, in particular, were fond of creating dinner parties with finger food and canapes increasingly appearing on the menu. Fondue, in particular, was a significant trend, where adults would hang out together and dip pieces of bread, meat, vegetables, and sometimes fruit into the large pots of melted cheese. Wine, hot cheese, and a game of bingo would be a typical night of fun for adults.

Chapter VI: Births & Deaths 1973

Births (onthisday.com)

Robin Dale Meyers – January 1st – American actress

Rahul Dravid – January 11th – Indian Cricketer

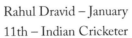

Giancarlo Fisichella – January 14th – Italian F1 Driver

Queen Mathilde of Belgium – January 20th – Queen of the Belgians

Oscar de la Hoya – February 4th – American Boxer

Cathy Freeman – February 16th – Australian Athlete

Claude Makélélé – February 18th – French Footballer

Julio Iglesias Jr. – February 25th – Spanish Singer

Ole Gunnar Solskjaer – February 26th – Norwegian Footballer and Manager

Peter Andre – February 27th – English Singer

Eva Herzigová – March 10th – Czech-Italian Supermodel

Caroline Corr – March 17th – Irish Singer

March 13th - Andy Bean: American Golfer

Jim Parsons – March 24th – American Actor

Stephen Fleming – April 1st – New Zealand Cricketer

David Blaine – April 4th – American Magician

Adrien Brody – April 14th – American Actor

Haile Gebrselassie - April 18th – Ethiopian Athlete

Jorge Garcia – April 28th – American Actor

Dario Franchitti – May 19th – Scottish Racing Driver

Heidi Klum – June 1st – German-American Supermodel

Neil Patrick Harris – June 15th – American Actor

Peter Kay – July 2nd – British Comedian

Monica Lewinsky – July 23rd – White House Intern

Kate Beckinsale – July 26th – British Actress

Greg Rusedski – September 6th – Canadian and British Tennis Player

Paul Walker – September 12th – American Actor

Eddie George – September 24th – American College Running Back Player

Peter Dumbreck – October 13th – Scottish Racing Driver

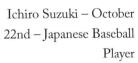

Ichiro Suzuki – October 22nd – Japanese Baseball Player

Seth MacFarlane – October 26th – Actor, Screenwriter, Producer and Director

Ryan Giggs – November 29th – Welsh Footballer

Monica Seles – December 2nd – Yugoslav/American Tennis Player

Paula Radcliffe – December 17th – English Athlete

Seth Meyers – December 28th – American Actor

Deaths (onthisday.com)

Lyndon B. Johnson – January 22nd – 36th American President

Edward G. Robinson – January 26th – Romanian-American Actor

Johannes Hans Daniel Jensen – February 11th - German Nuclear Physicist

Frank Costello – February 18th – Italian-American Crime Boss

Noel Coward – March 26th – British Playwright

Pablo Picasso – April 8th – Spanish Painter

Arna Bontemps – June 4th
– American Poet

 Nancy Mitford – June 30th
– British Writer

 Betty Grable – July 2nd –
American Actress

 Bruce Lee – July 20th –
Hong Kong and American
Actor and Martial Artist

 Louis St. Laurent – July
25th – 12th Prime Minister
of Canada

 Roger Williamson – July
29th – English Racing
Driver

 Fulgencio Batista – August
6th – Cuba President

 John Ford – August 31st –
American Film Director

 J. R. R. Tolkien –
September 2nd – English
Writer

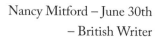

Chapter VII: Statistics 1973

* US GDP 1973 – 5.69 trillion US $ (worldbank.org)

* US GDP 2021 – 22.9 trillion US $ (worldbank.org)

* UK GDP 1973 – 169.97 billion US $ (worldbank.org)

* UK GDP 2021 – 3.19 trillion US $ (worldbank.org)

* US Inflation – 1973 (worldbank.org) – 5.5%

* US Inflation – 2021 (worldbank.org) – 4.2%

* UK. Inflation – 1973 (worldbank.org) – 9.2%

* UK Inflation – 2021 (worldbank.org) – 2.5%

* U.S. Population – 1973 – 201,909,000 (worldbank.org)

* U.S. Population – 2021 – 331, 893, 775 (worldbank.org)

* UK. Population – 1973 – 56,194, 527 (worldbank.org)

* UK. Population – 2021 – 67,326,579 (worldbank.org)

* U.S. Life Expectancy At Birth 1973 – 71 (worldbank.org)

* U.S. Life Expectancy At Birth 2021 – 77 (worldbank.org)

* U.K. Life Expectancy At Birth 1973 – 71 (worldbank.org)

* U.K. Life Expectancy At Birth 2020 – 81 (worldbank.org)

* U.S. Unemployment Rate 1973 – 9.0% (zippia.com)

* U.S. Unemployment Rate 2021 – 3.9%(thebalance.com)

* U.K. Unemployment Rate 1973– 3.4% (fxempire.com)

⋆ U.K. Unemployment Rate 2022 – 3.8% (ons.gov.uk)

⋆ U.S. Total Tax Revenue 1973 – 231 billion USD (thebalance.com)

⋆ U.S. Total Tax Revenue 2022 – 2.6 trillion USD (businessinsider.com)

⋆ U.K. Total Tax Revenue 1973 – 32.45 billion (ukpublicrevenue.co.uk)

⋆ U.K. Total Tax Revenue 2022 – 178.4 billion (gov.uk)

⋆ U.S. Prison Population 1973 – 218,466 (sentencingproject.com)

⋆ U.S. Prison Population 2022 – 2.1 million (sentencingproject.com)

⋆ U.K. Prison Population 1973 – 37,692 (parliament.uk)

⋆ U.K. Prison Population 2020 – 12,747 (prisonstudies.org)

⋆ Average cost of new house 1973 US – $32,500 (huduser.gov)

⋆ Average Cost of new house US 2022 – $348,000 (gobankingrates.com)

⋆ Average cost of new house 1973 UK – £9,045 (loveproperty.com)

⋆ Average Cost of new house 2022 UK – £296,000 (ons.gov.uk)

⋆ Average income per year 1973 US – $10,300 (census.gov)

⋆ Average income per year 2022 US – $106,000 (worldpopulationreview.com)

⋆ Average income per year 1973 UK – £1,981 (gov.uk)

⋆ Average income per year 2022 UK – £37,922 (gov.uk)

Cost Of Things

In 1973, the cost of various things, be it a house or a loaf of bread, was considerably different to what people would pay in 2022. Here are some of the prices charged for various items in 1973:

United States:

 ✯ Fresh eggs (1 dozen): $0.78 (stacker.com)

 ✯ White bread (1 pound): $0.28 (stacker.com)

 ✯ Sliced bacon (1 pound): $1.33 (stacker.com)

 ✯ Round steak (1 pound): $1.75 (stacker.com)

 ✯ Potatoes (10 pounds): $1.37 (stacker.com)

 ✯ Fresh delivered milk (1/2 gallon): $0.69 (stacker.com)

 ✯ Average Price Of A Car - $3,415 (cheapism.com)

 ✯ Average Price Of A Gallon Of Petrol - $0.39 (titlemax.com)

United Kingdom (retrowow.co.uk):

 ✯ Gallon of petrol - £0,39

 ✯ Bottle of whisky (Haig) (Co-op) - £2,45

 ✯ Pint of beer - £0,185

 ✯ 20 cigarettes - £0,265

 ✯ Pint of milk - £0,055

 ✯ Large loaf of bread - £0,115

 ✯ One dozen large white eggs - £0,32

 ✯ 1lb Stork Soft margarine (Tesco) - £0,125

 ✯ Nescafé 8oz coffee (Tesco) - £0,54

* Can of Coke (Mac Markets) - £0,055

* The Daily Mirror newspaper - £0,03

* Polaris refridgerator (Currys) - £30.95

* 22" Pye colour TV (Currys) - £208.90

* 24" Ferguson black & white TV (Currys) - £61.75

* Ford Cortina car - £1,075

Chapter VIII: Iconic Advertisements of 1973

Ford: 1973 Mercury Montego

Winchester

IBM: Correcting Selectric Typewriter

Clairol: Herbal Essence Shampoo

Gordon's Gin

Converse: All Star

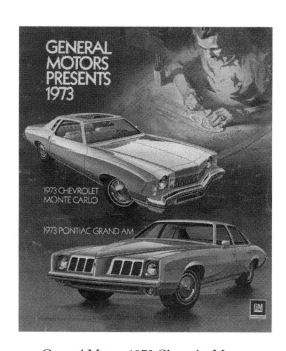

General Motor: 1973 Chevrolet Monte
Carlo & 1973 Pontiac Grand AM

Coca-Cola

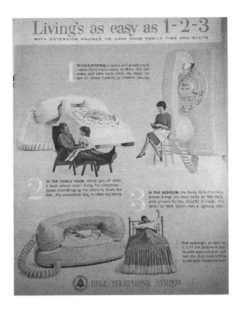

Bell Telephone System

Vitalis: Dry Control

Campbell's Tomato Soup

General Electric: Portable Room Air
Conditioner

Chrysler Corvette

Philips: Radio Recorders

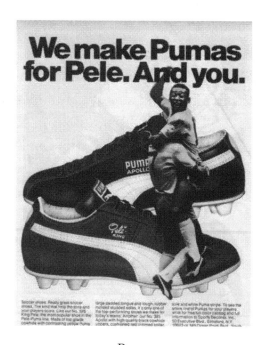

Puma

Johnson & Johnson: Baby Shampoo

Pan Am

De Tomaso Pantera L

Virginia Slims

7 Up

Kodak: Pocket Instamatic Camera

Jose Cuervo Tequila

Automatic, at last.

Together for the first time. You and the only station wagon in the world with 176 cubic feet of carrying space. 4-wheel independent suspension, and a fully automatic transmission.

The 1973 Volkswagen Station Wagon. Now with automatic transmission. Mommy's big helper.

Volkswagen

Tires for a movin' van.

Van tires know you need a wide road gripper to turn on a trick West Coast job. Firestone's Hard Chargers really do it. They corner, steer, stop and stick to the road. And they have Firestone's 61 years of racing experience behind them. That's how all of Firestone's Hard Chargers are alike. Now see your Firestone Dealer or Store and find out how different each one is.

the hard chargers from Firestone

Firestone

Algunos televisores de colores lo hacen a uno trabajar. Este deja que uno vea sin molestias.

El CT-960 de Hitachi se proyectó para quienes prefieren ver programas de TV en colores en vez de estar ajustando el televisor. Porque contiene 11 dispositivos que ajustan automáticamente la imagen.

Dispositivos tales como un bolen, exclusivo de Hitachi, que permite ajustar en una operación el tono, la densidad, la luminosidad y el contraste.

Características tales como el Control Automático de la Frecuencia. Dos circuitos distintos para Control Automático de Ganancia. Dos reguladores de voltaje independientes. Un compensador automático de interferencia y un limitador automático de luminosidad. Para no mencionar los circuitos de AHFC, ACC y ACK. Y el atractivo soporte giratorio que viene con el CT-960.

Quizá usted esté bien explicado estas características, pero preferimos que lo haga uno de nuestros agentes. Y mientras él explica usted podrá estar viendo, porque viendo es como uno se divierte.

HITACHI

Hitachi

Atlas

INDIA'S LARGEST SELLING BICYCLE

Atlas

Sony: Portable Stereo Cassette-Corder
AM/FM Radio Combination

Marlboro

I have a gift for you!

Dear reader, thank you so much for reading my book!

To make this book more (much more!) affordable, the images are all black & white, but I've created a special gift for you!

You can now have access, for FREE, to the PDF version of this book with the original images!

Keep in mind that some are originally black & white, but a lot of them are colored.

I hope you enjoy it!

Download it here:

http://bit.ly/3gAzwqj

Or Scan this QR Code:

I have a favor to ask you!

I deeply hope you've enjoyed reading this book and felt transported right into 1973!

I loved researching it, organizing it, and writing it, knowing that it would make your day a little brighter.

If you've enjoyed it too, I would be extremely grateful if you took just a few minutes to leave a positive customer review and share it with your friends.

As an unknown author, that makes all the difference and gives me the extra energy I need to keep researching, writing, and bringing joy to all my readers. Thank you!

Best regards,
Robert E. Miller

Please leave a positive book review here:

http://bit.ly/3U8IR6q

Or Scan this QR Code:

Check Our Other Books!

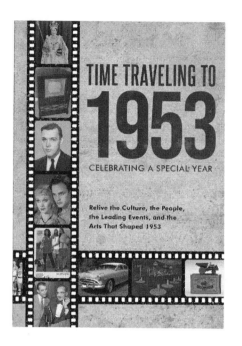

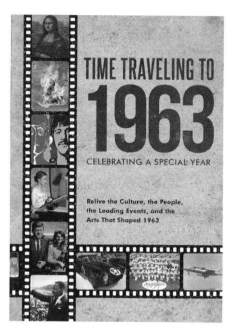

Made in the USA
Middletown, DE
10 February 2023

24527346R00060